WIND

BY HARRIET BRUNDLE

Enslow PUBLISHING

Weather Explorers

Weather
Explorers

Please visit our website, www.enslow.com. For a free color catalog of all our high-quality books, call toll free 1-800-398-2504 or fax 1-877-980-4454.

Cataloging-in-Publication Data

Names: Brundle, Harriet.
Title: Wind / Harriet Brundle.
Description: New York : Enslow Publishing, 2021. | Series: Weather explorers | Includes glossary and index.
Identifiers: ISBN 9781978520660 (pbk.) | ISBN 9781978520684 (library bound) | ISBN 9781978520677 (6 pack)
Subjects: LCSH: Winds--Juvenile literature. | Weather--Juvenile literature.
Classification: LCC QC931.4 B78 2021 | DDC 551.51'8--dc23

Published in 2021 by
Enslow Publishing
101 West 23rd Street, Suite #240
New York, NY 10011

Manufactured in the United States of America

CPSIA compliance information: Batch #BS20ENS: For further information contact Enslow Publishing, New York, New York, at 1-800-398-2504.

CONTENTS

Words in **bold** can be found in the glossary on page 24.

WIND

Wind is air that is moving around Earth.

Wind is sometimes a soft breeze, or it can be very strong and powerful.

SOFT BREEZE

HOW DOES WIND HAPPEN?

Some parts of Earth are very warm. Other parts do not get as much sunlight, so they are colder.

COLD PLACE

WARM PLACE

Air that is warmer rises up and colder air **replaces** it. This causes wind.

COLD AIR

WARM AIR

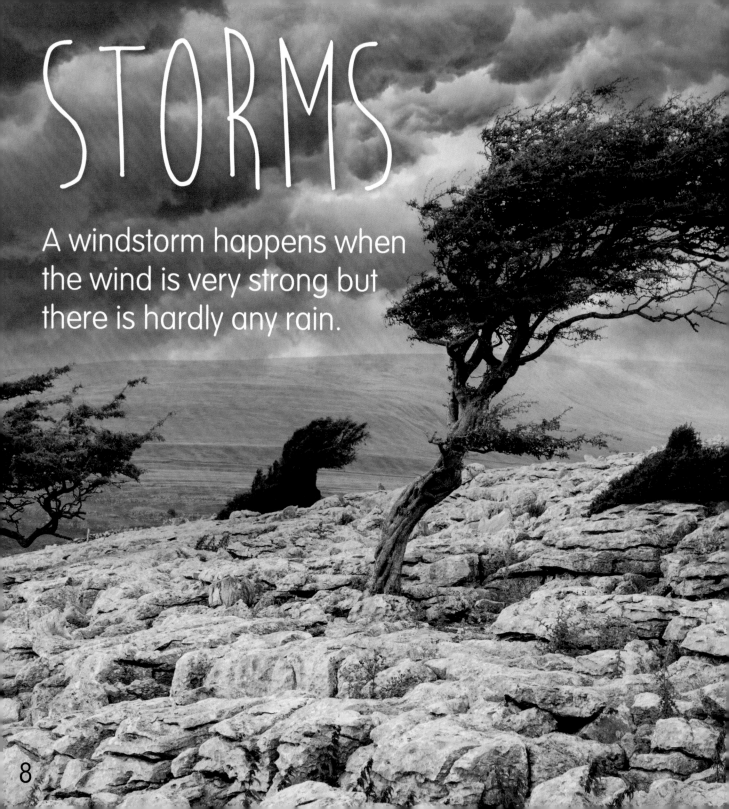

STORMS

A windstorm happens when the wind is very strong but there is hardly any rain.

When there is a thunderstorm, there will usually be strong winds and rain.

LIGHTNING

WIND AND THE SEASONS

There are four seasons in a year.

SPRING

SUMMER

WINTER

AUTUMN

Late winter and spring are the windiest times of the year in most of the United States.

There is often wind in the other seasons too.

When the weather is warm in the summertime, the wind helps to keep us cool.

WHAT DO WE WEAR?

When wind is very cold, we wear coats to keep warm.

It might be hard to wear a hat when it is windy. The wind could blow it away!

PLANTS

Wind can **damage** plants by breaking off their branches, leaves, or flowers.

FLOWER

SEEDS

Wind can also be helpful to plants. The wind blows seeds from some plants to new places. The seeds may land on the ground and start to grow.

17

ANIMALS

Birds use the wind
to glide when they
are flying.

This means they don't need to flap their wings as much. This helps them save energy.

GLIDING

DANGEROUS WIND

Some types of wind can be very dangerous. A hurricane is a very strong storm with fast winds and heavy rain.

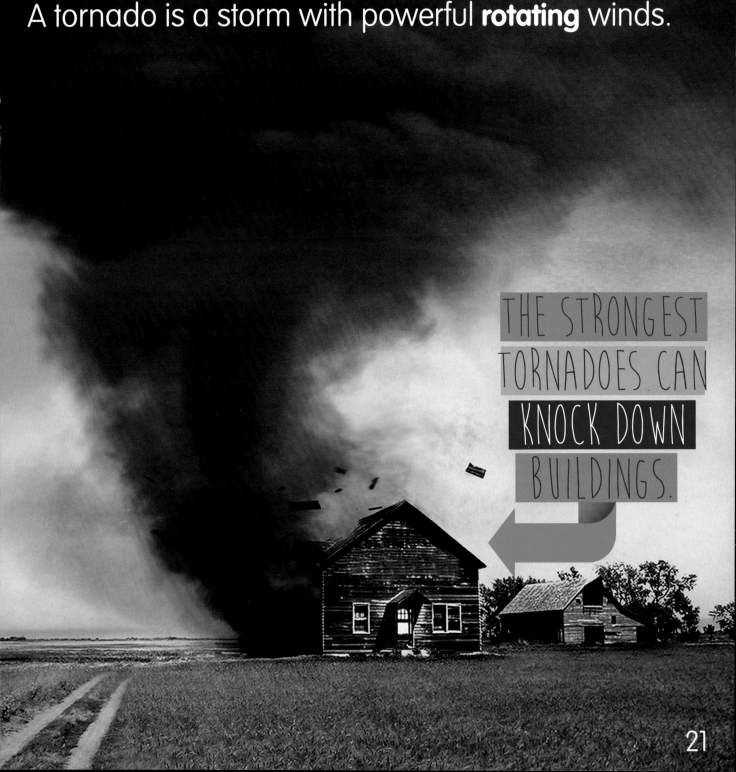

A tornado is a storm with powerful **rotating** winds.

THE STRONGEST TORNADOES CAN KNOCK DOWN BUILDINGS.

DID YOU KNOW?

People have used the wind to sail around Earth. The fastest sailing trip around Earth took just 42 days!

THE SPEED OF THE WIND CAN BE **MEASURED** IN KNOTS.

In some places on Earth, the wind can reach speeds faster than a race car!